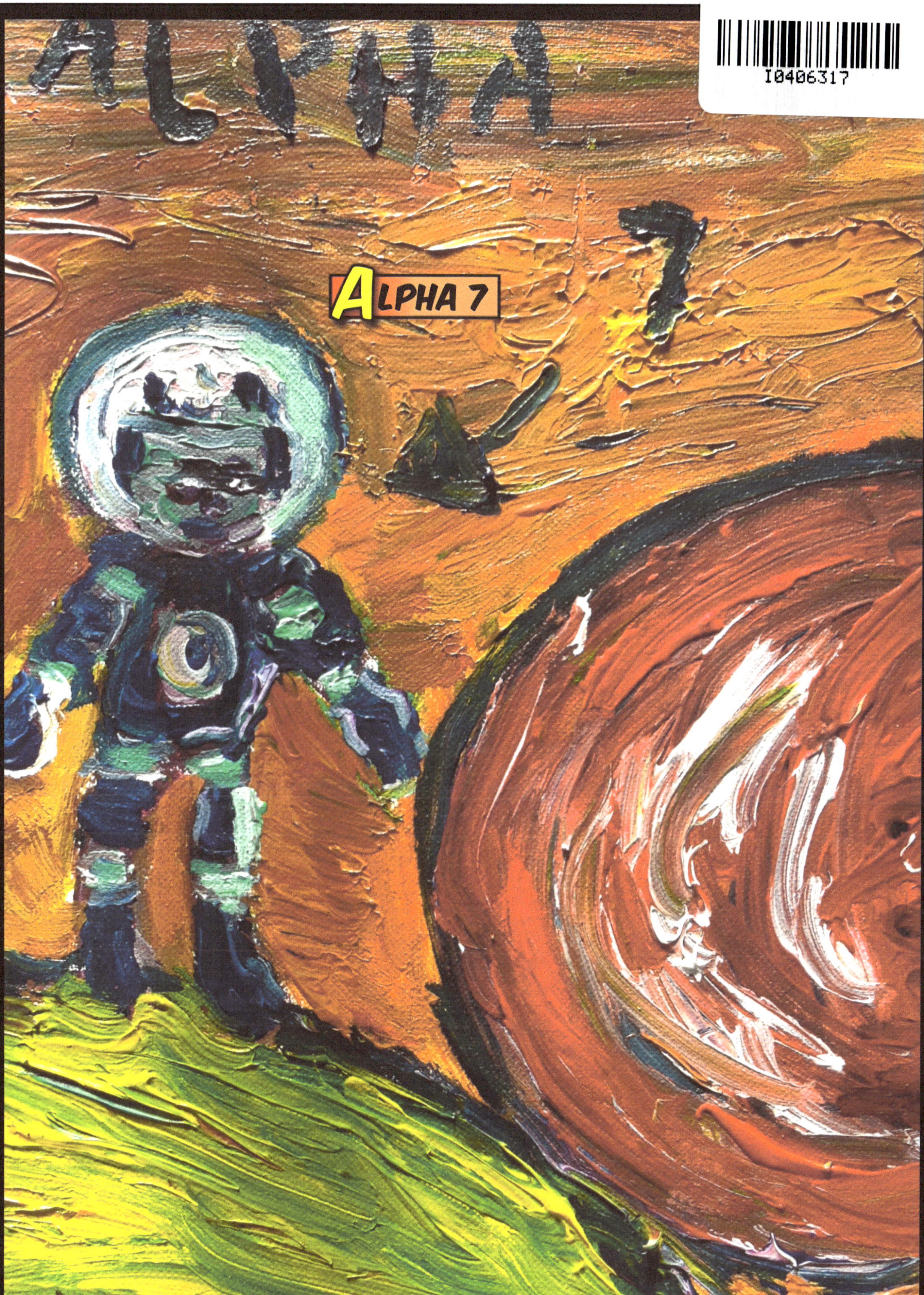

ALPHA 7

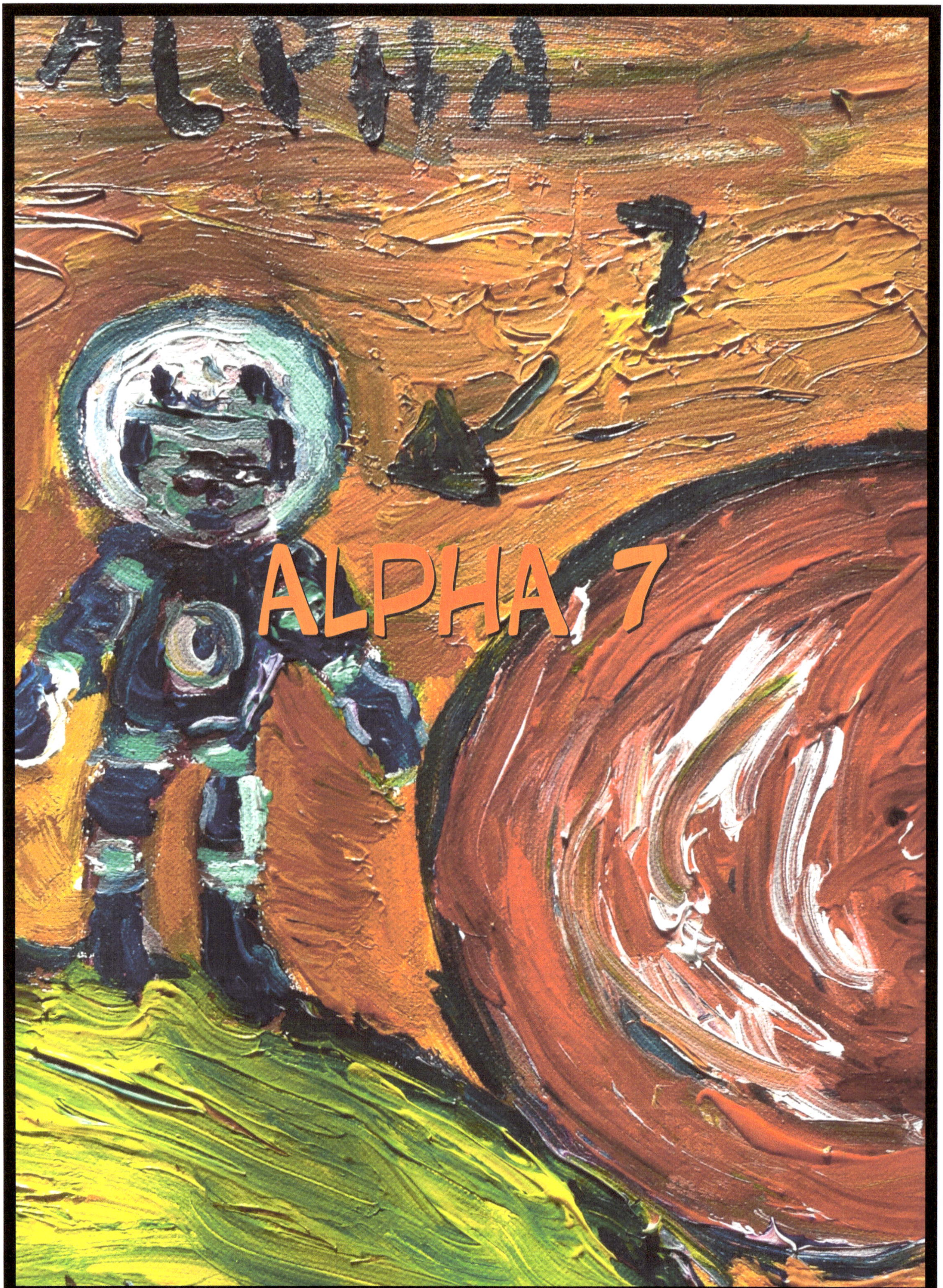
ALPHA
7
ALPHA 7

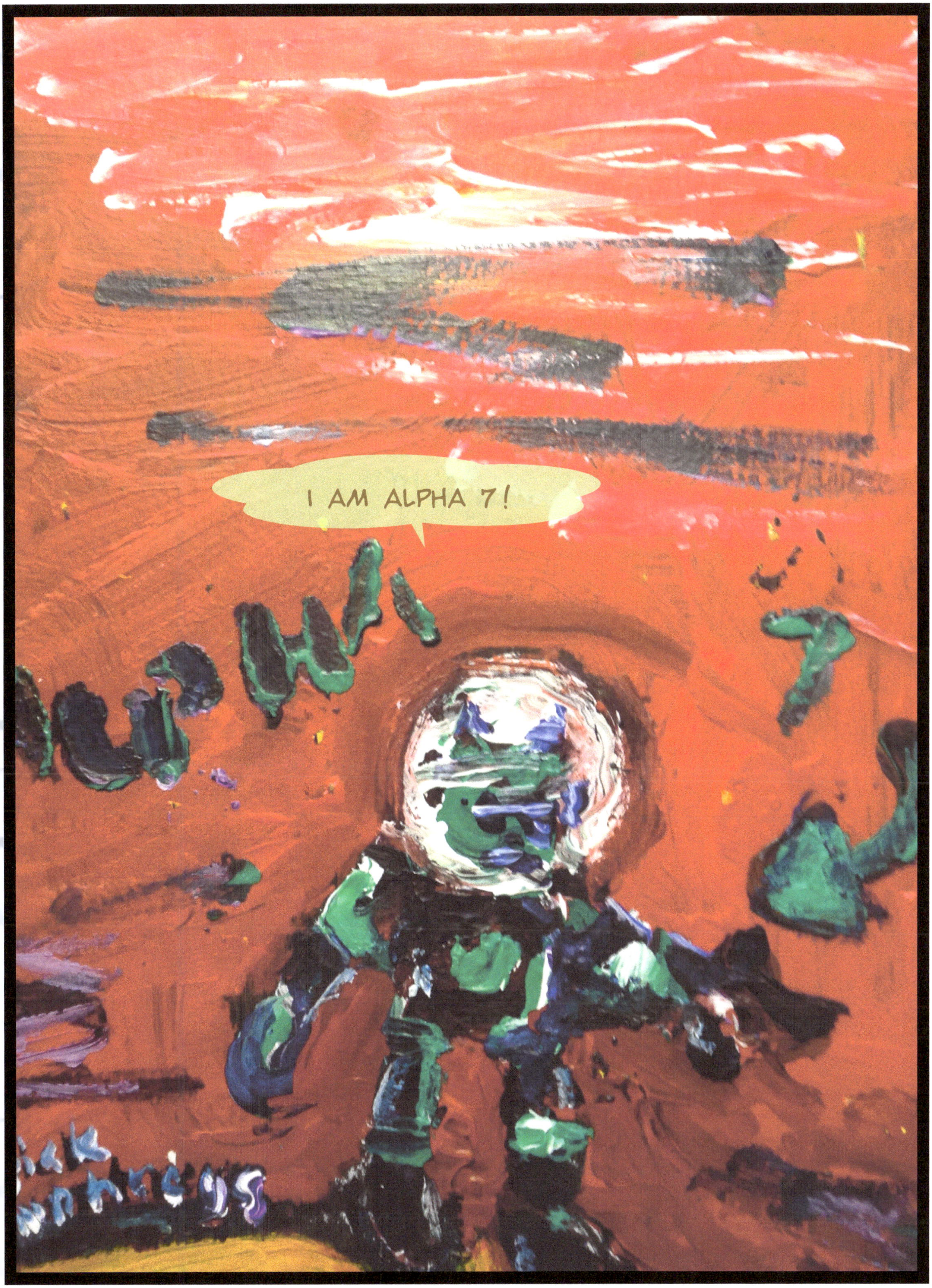
I AM ALPHA 7!

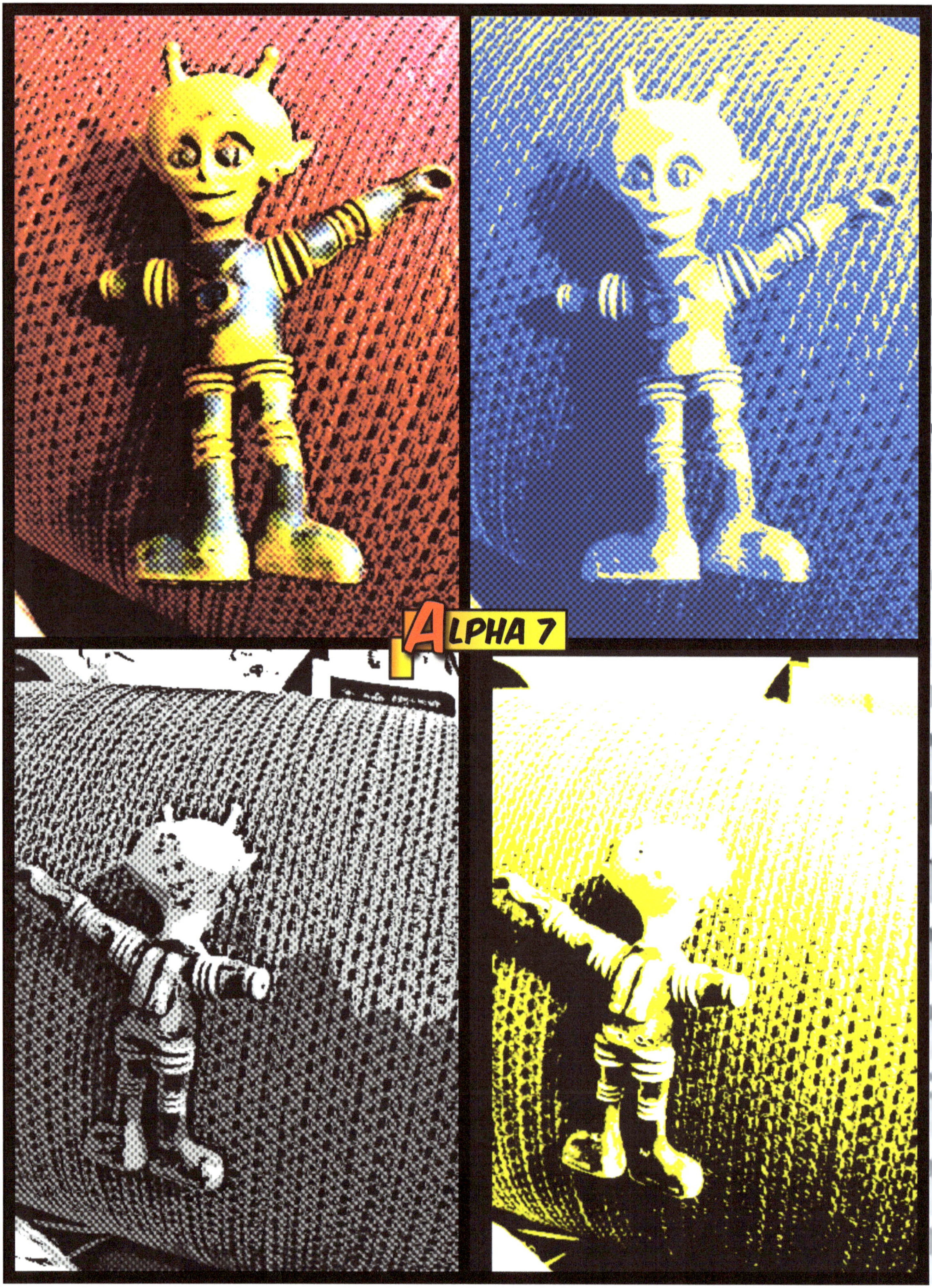
ALPHA 7

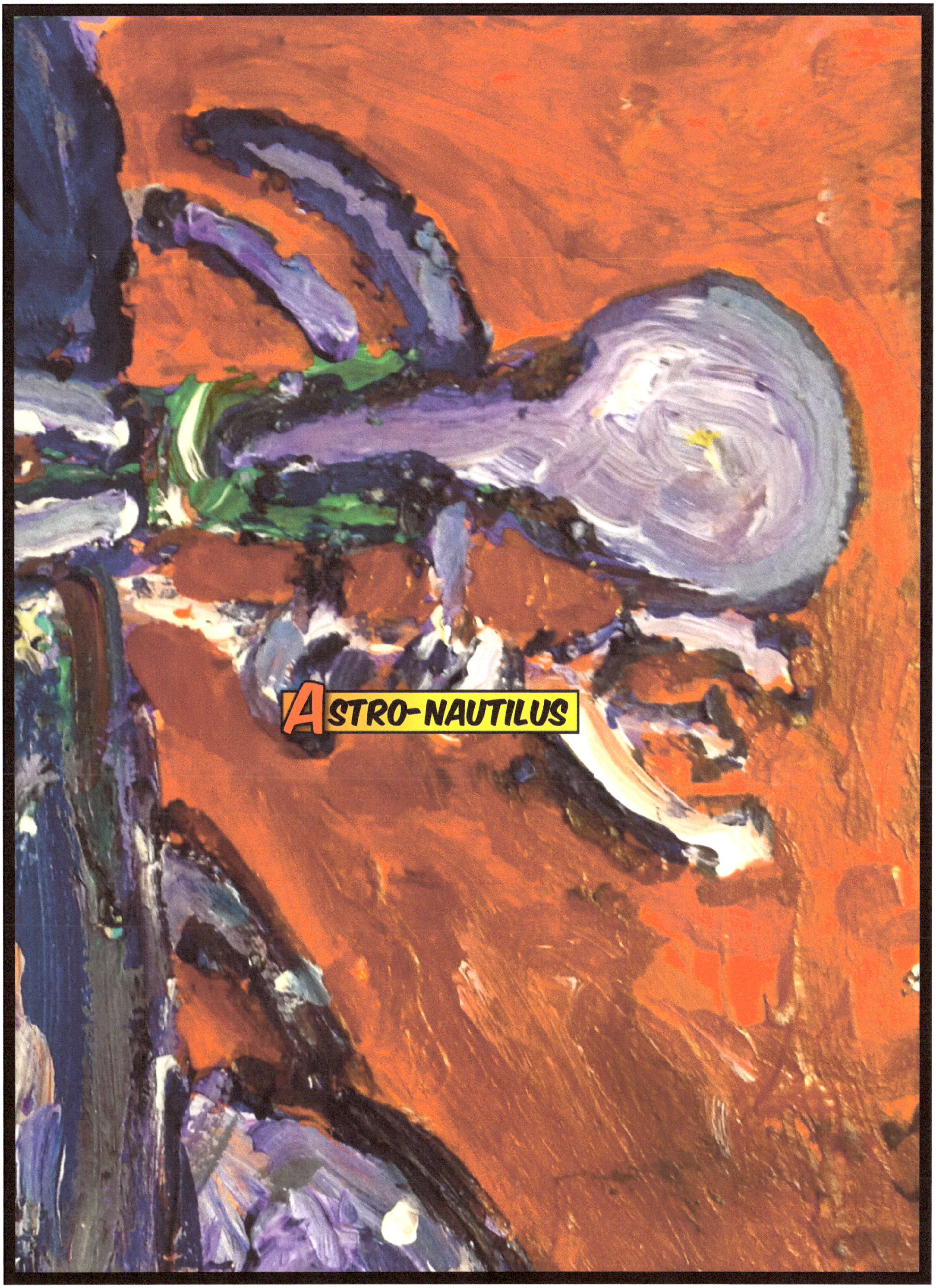
ASTRO-NAUTILUS

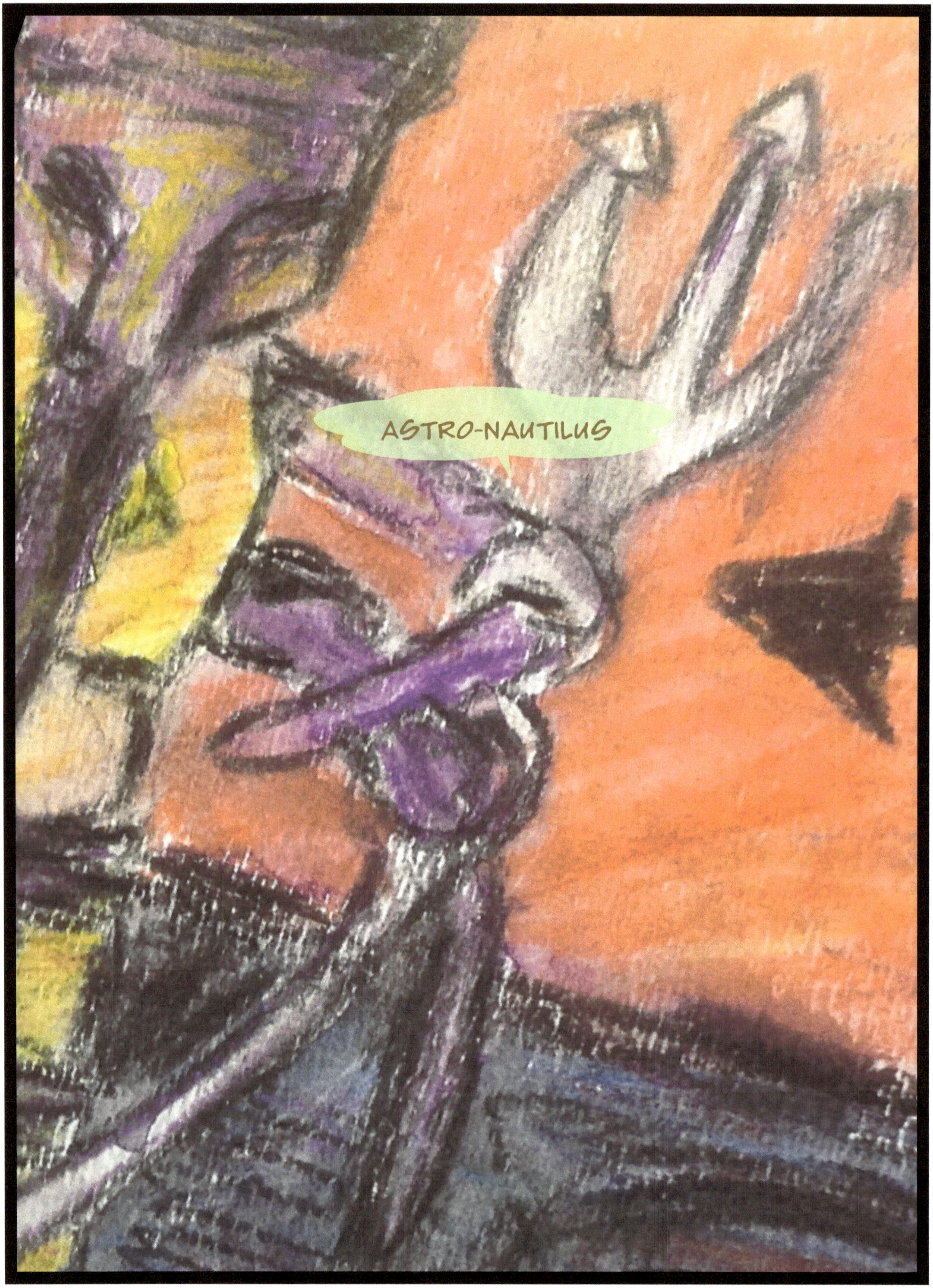
ASTRO-NAUTILUS

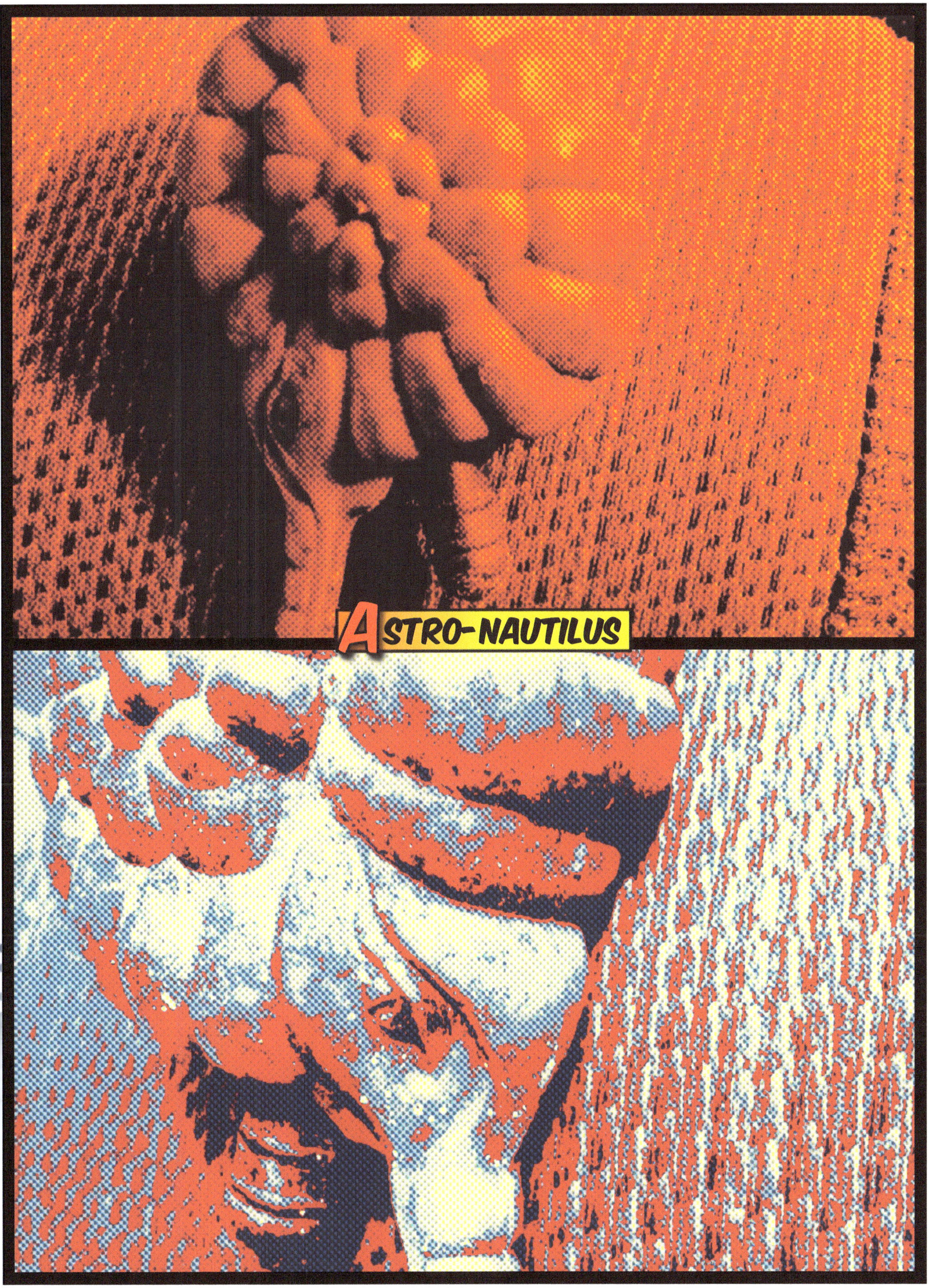
ASTRO-NAUTILUS

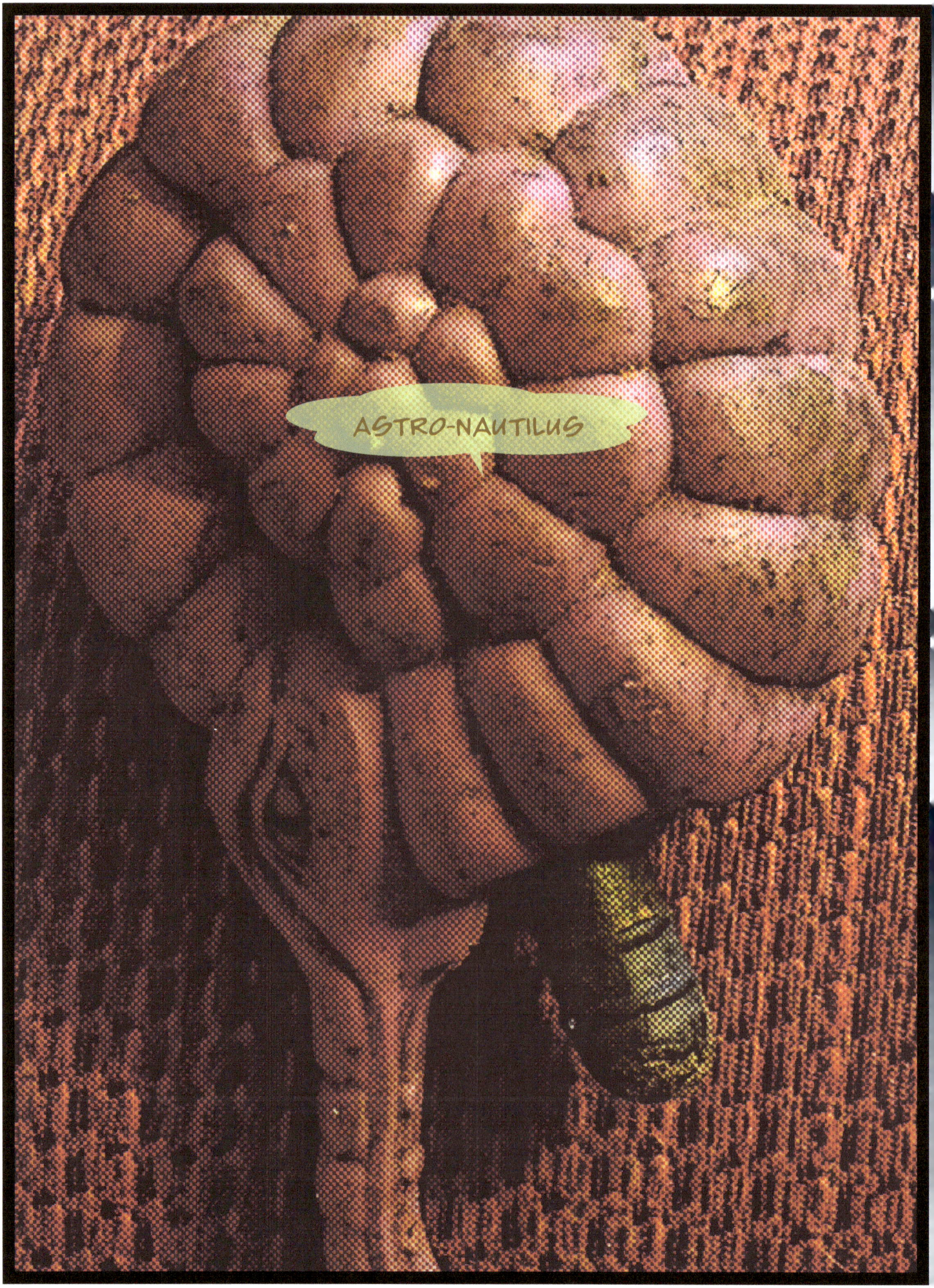
ASTRO-NAUTILUS

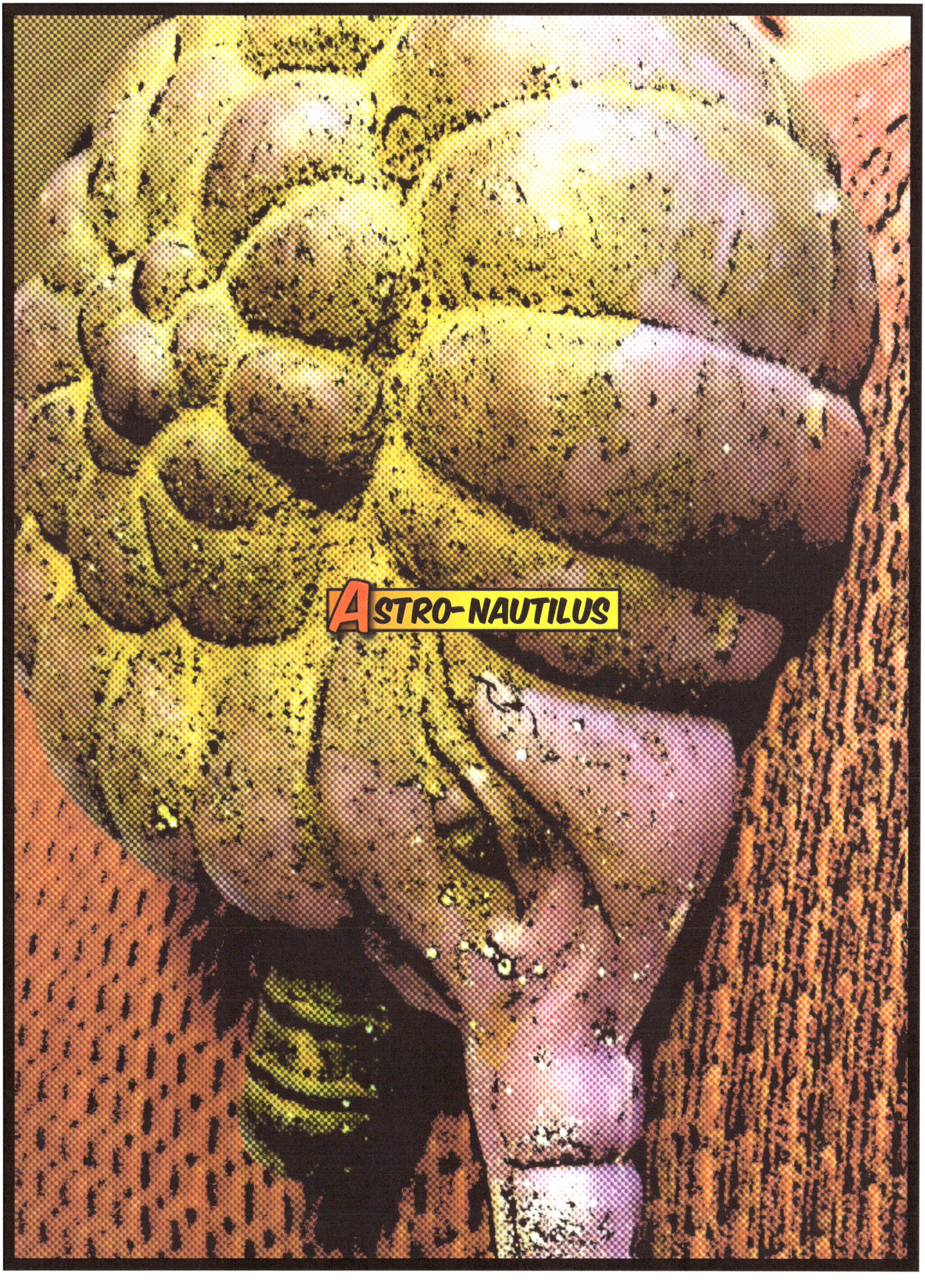
ASTRO-NAUTILUS

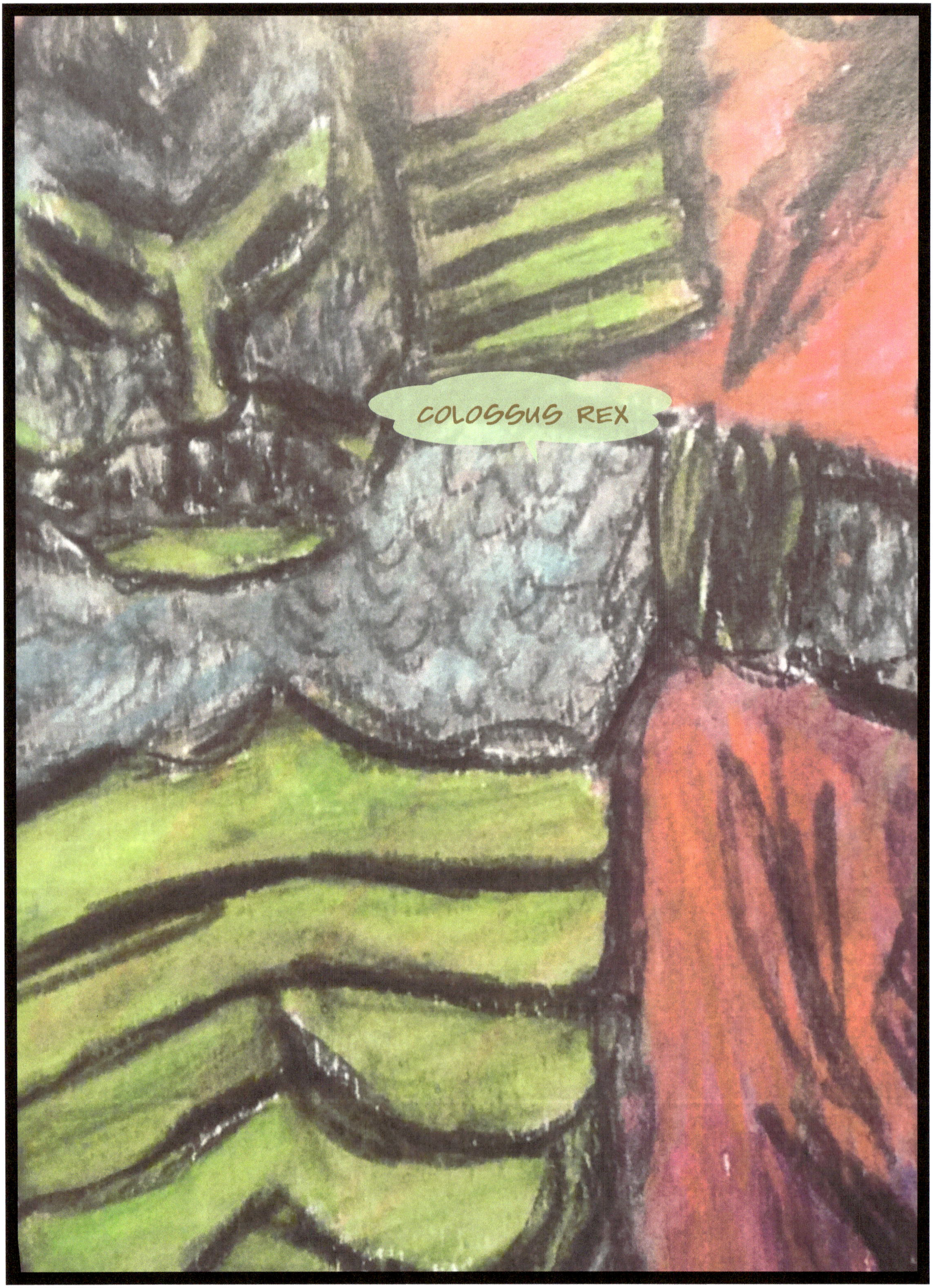
COLOSSUS REX

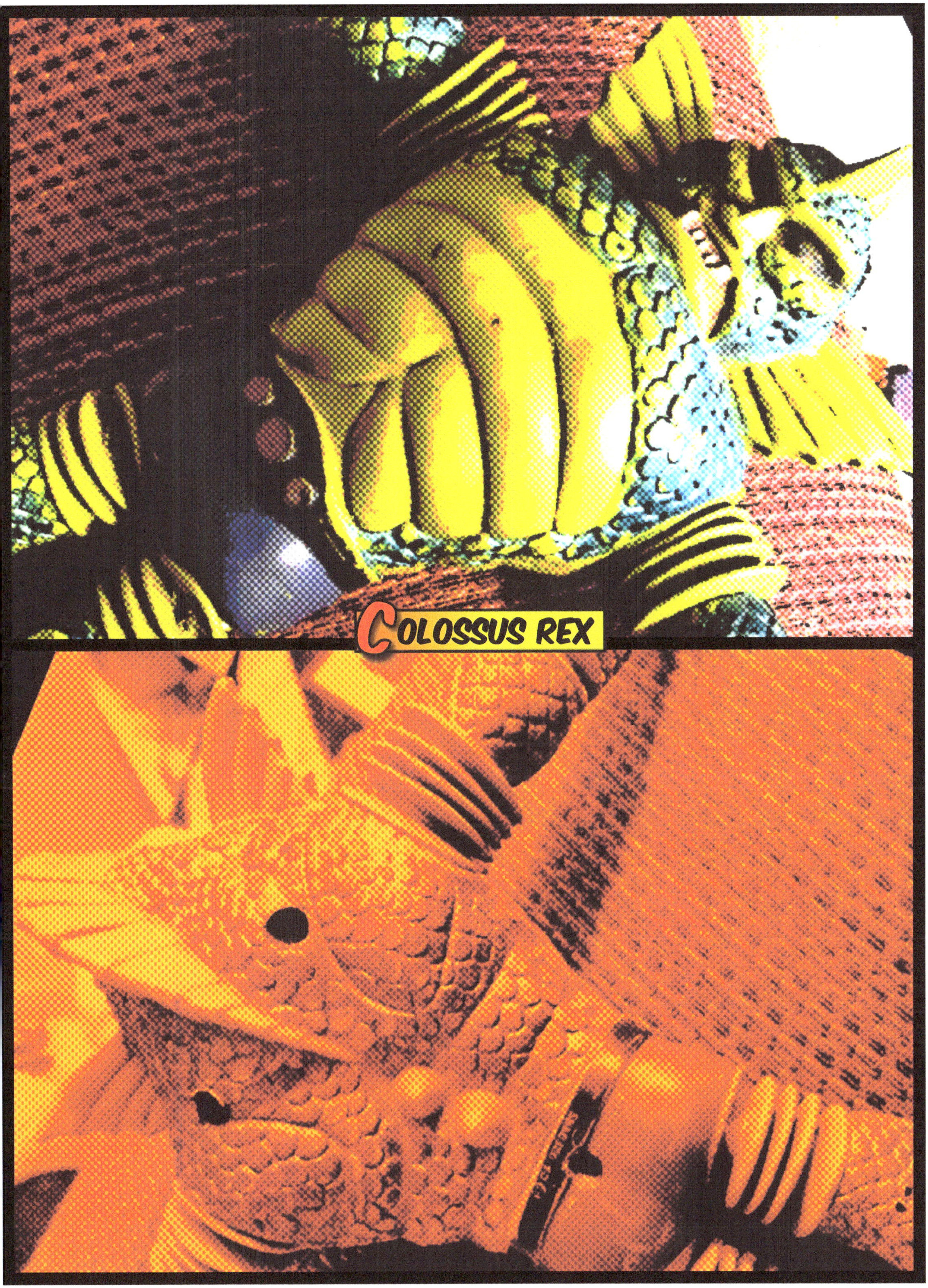
COLOSSUS REX

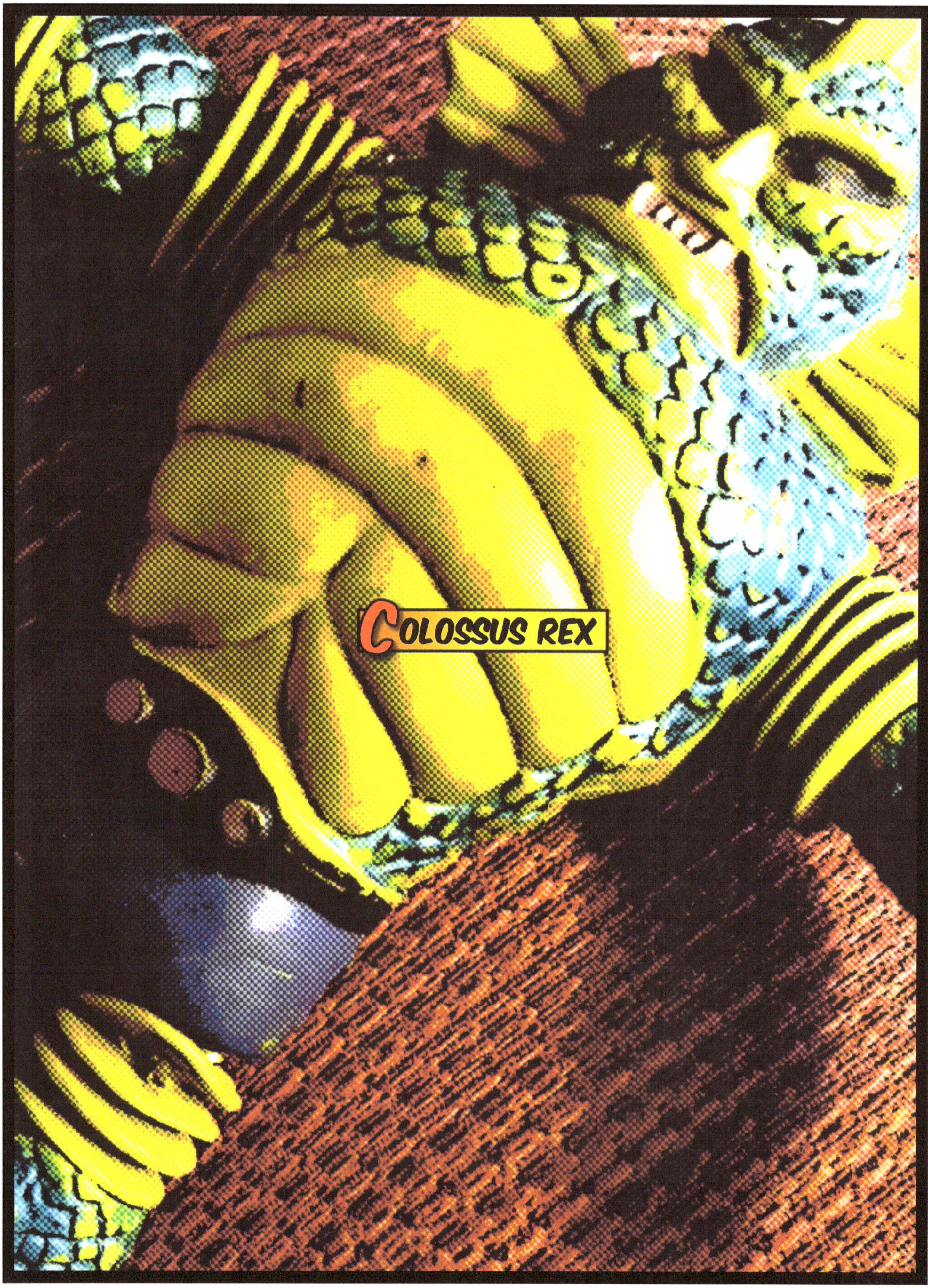
COLOSSUS REX

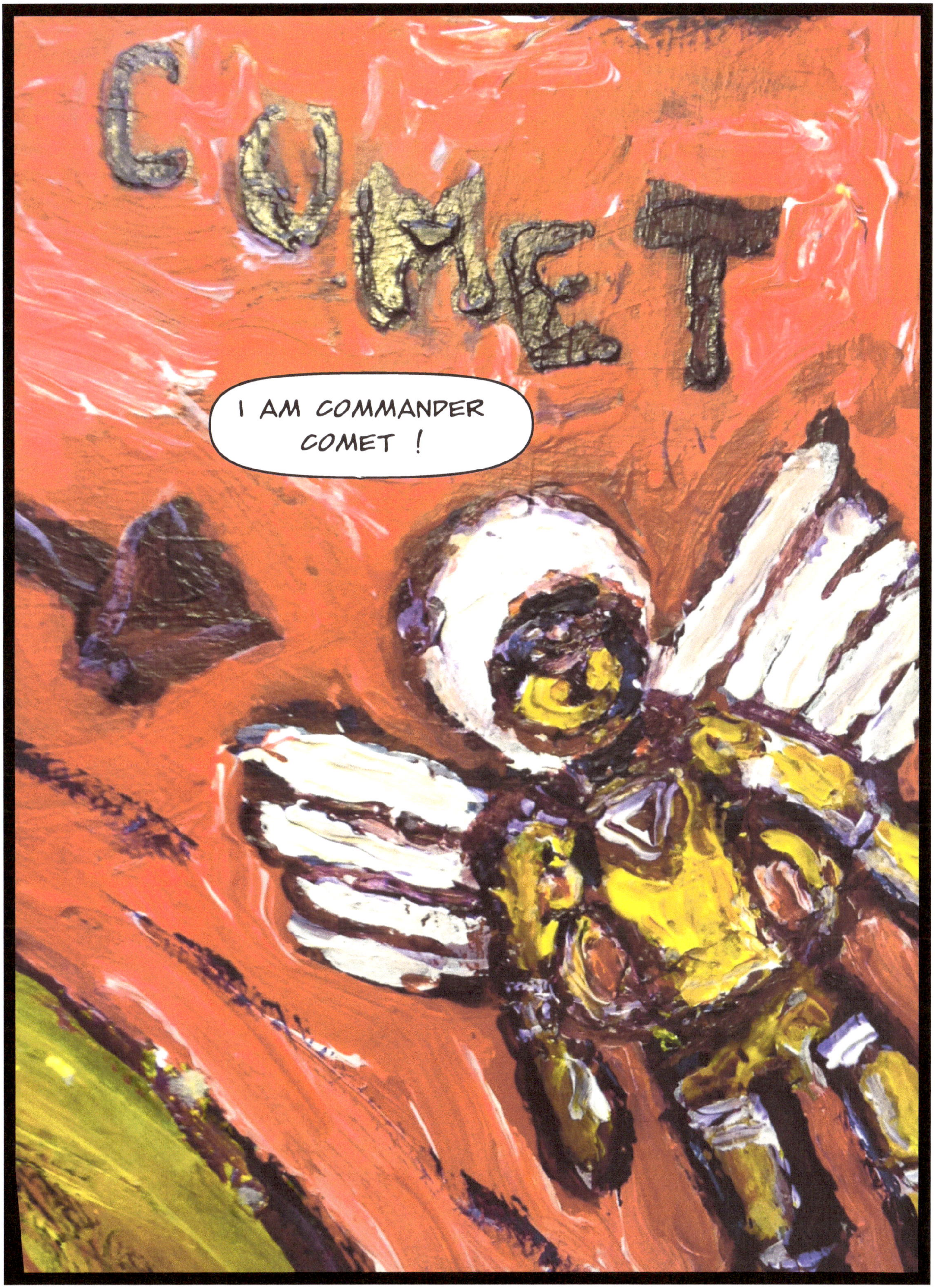
COMET
I AM COMMANDER COMET !

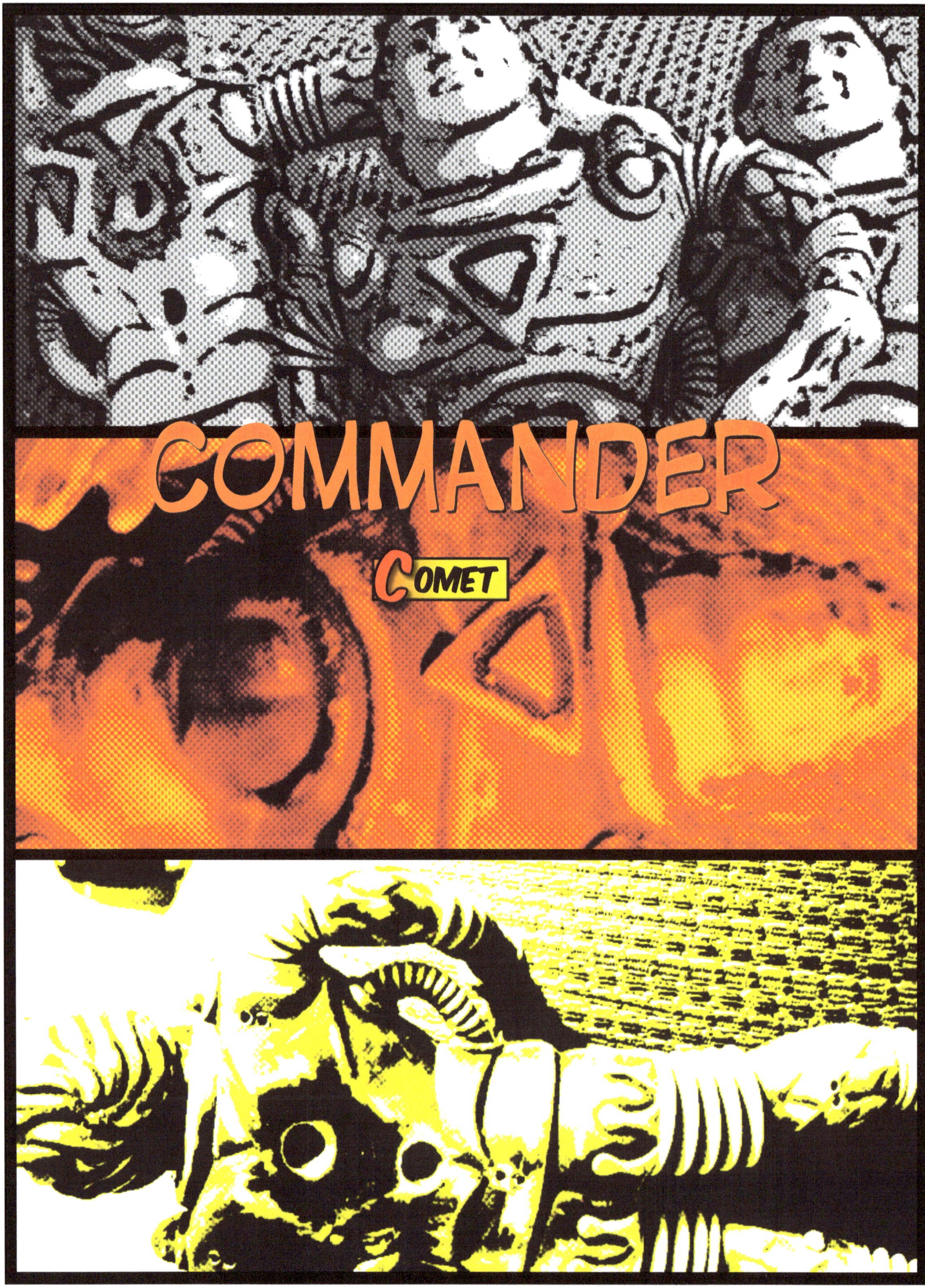
COMMANDER
COMET

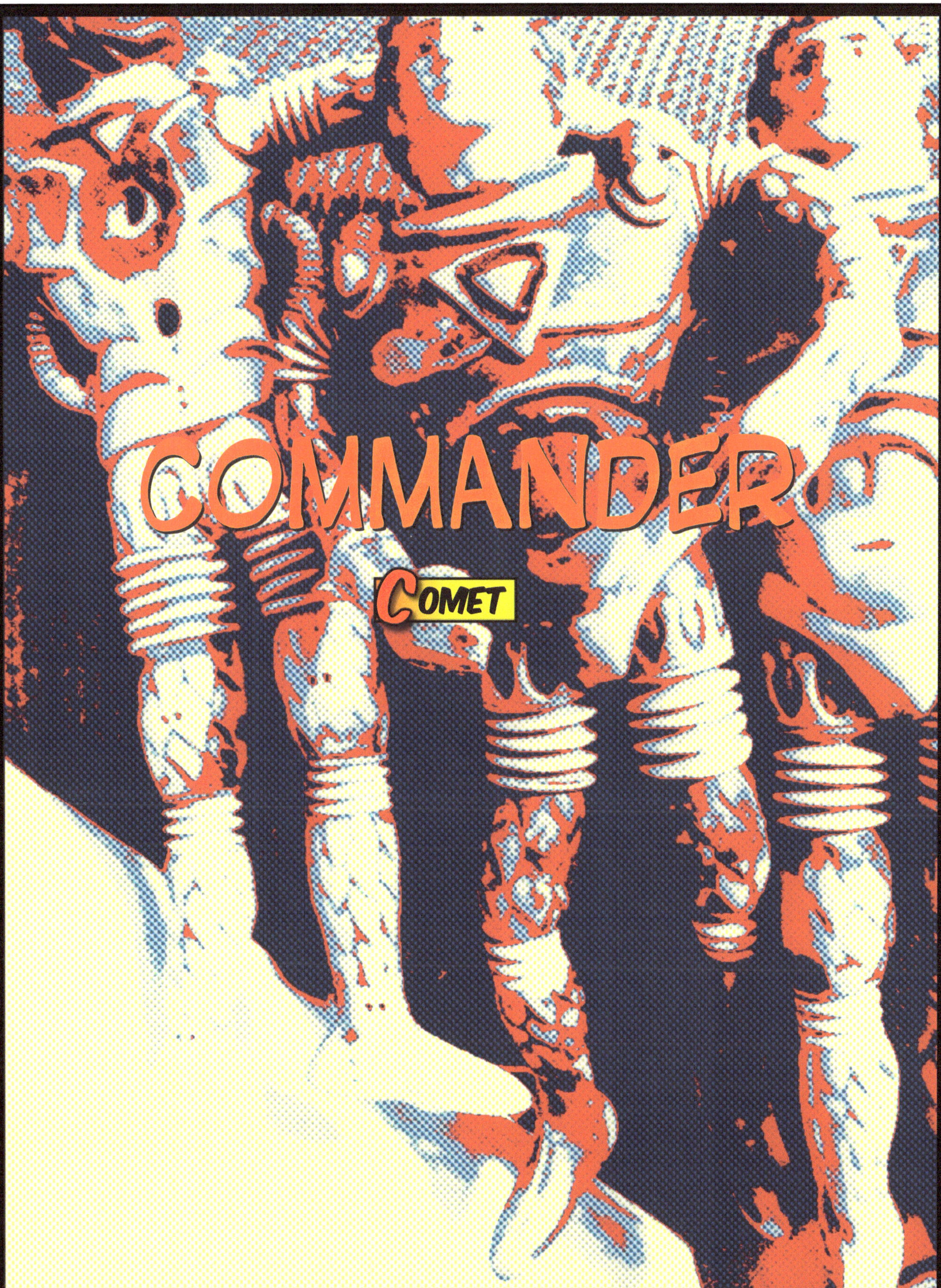
COMMANDER
COMET

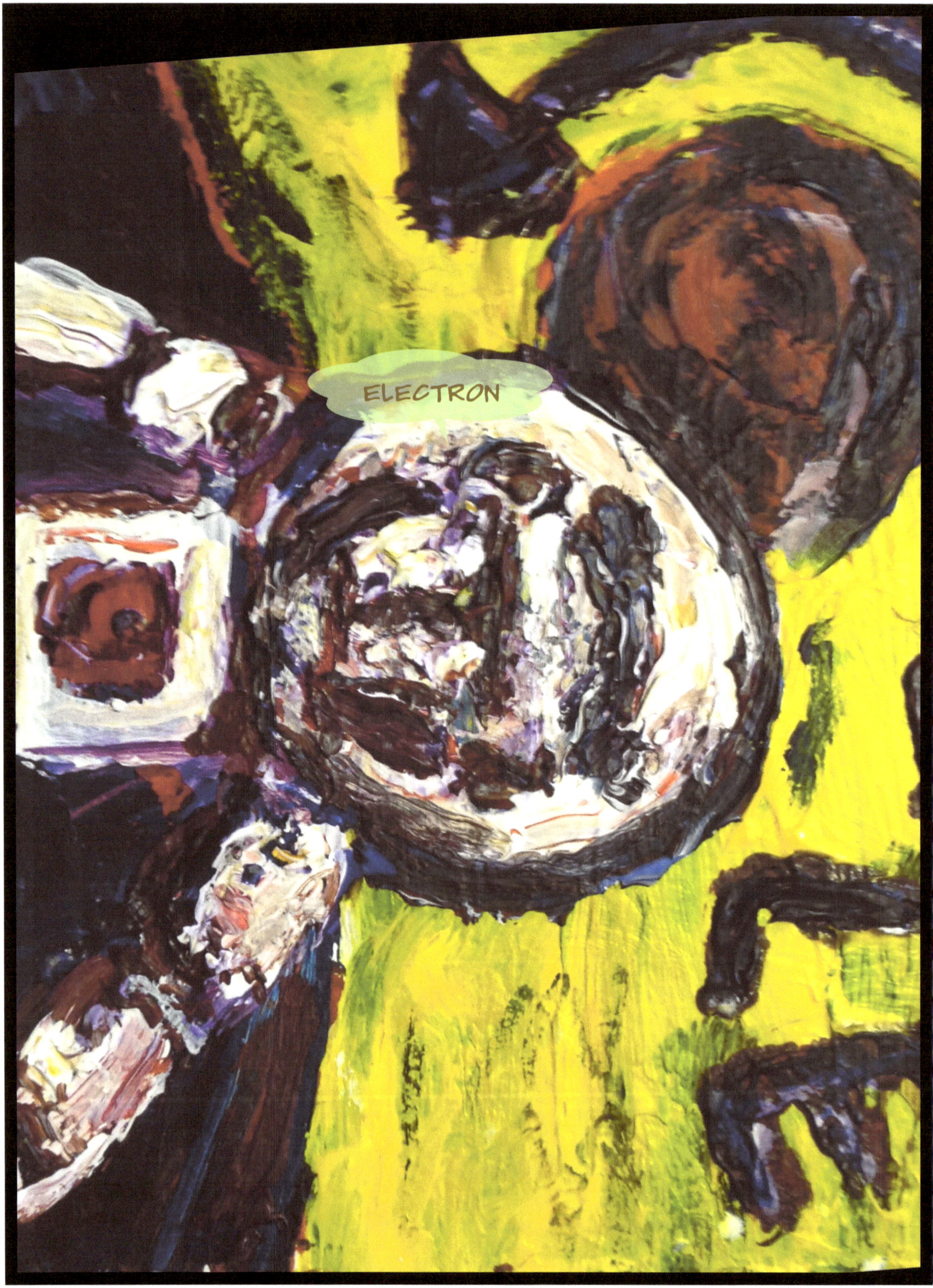
ELECTRON

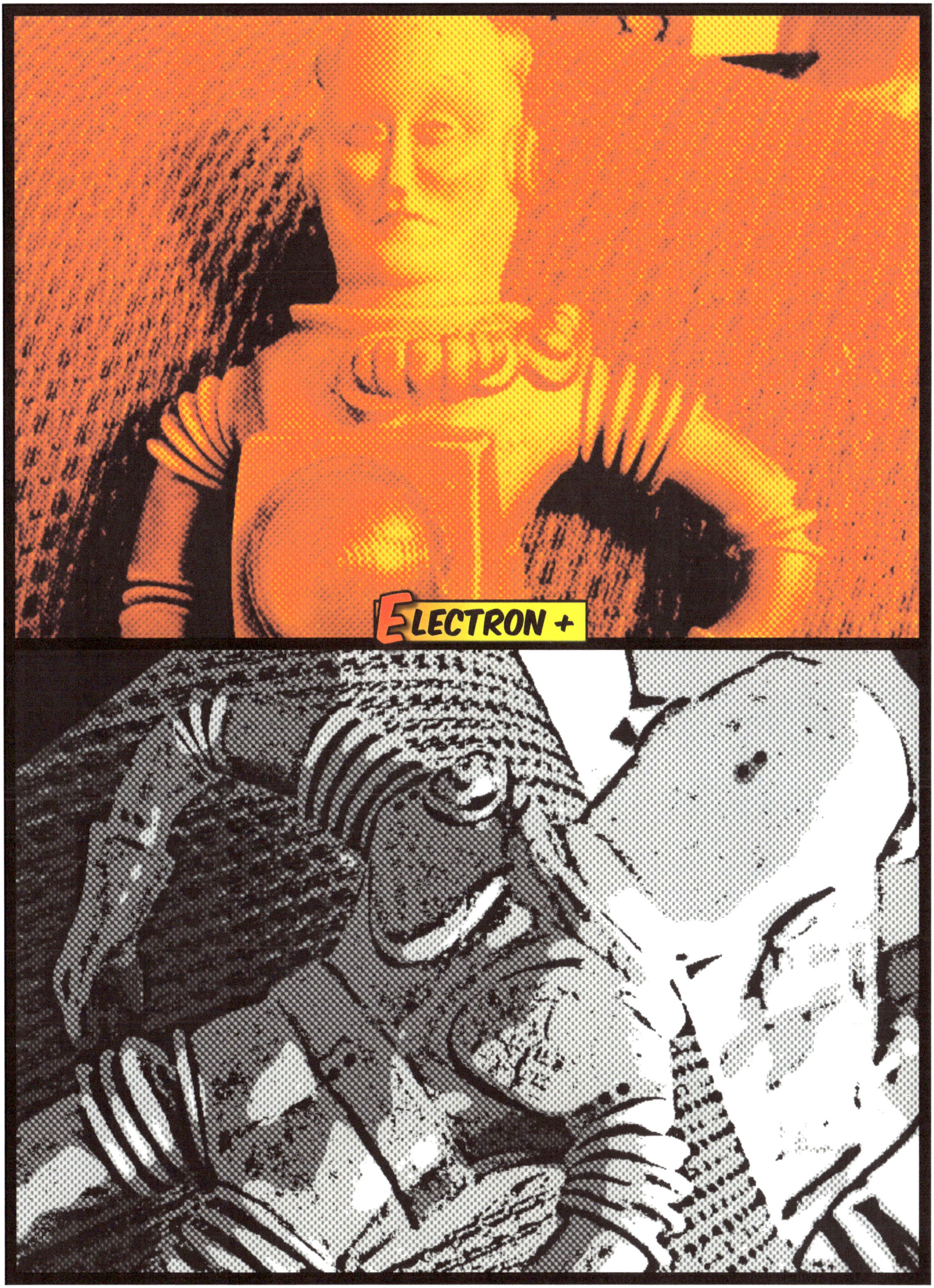
ELECTRON +

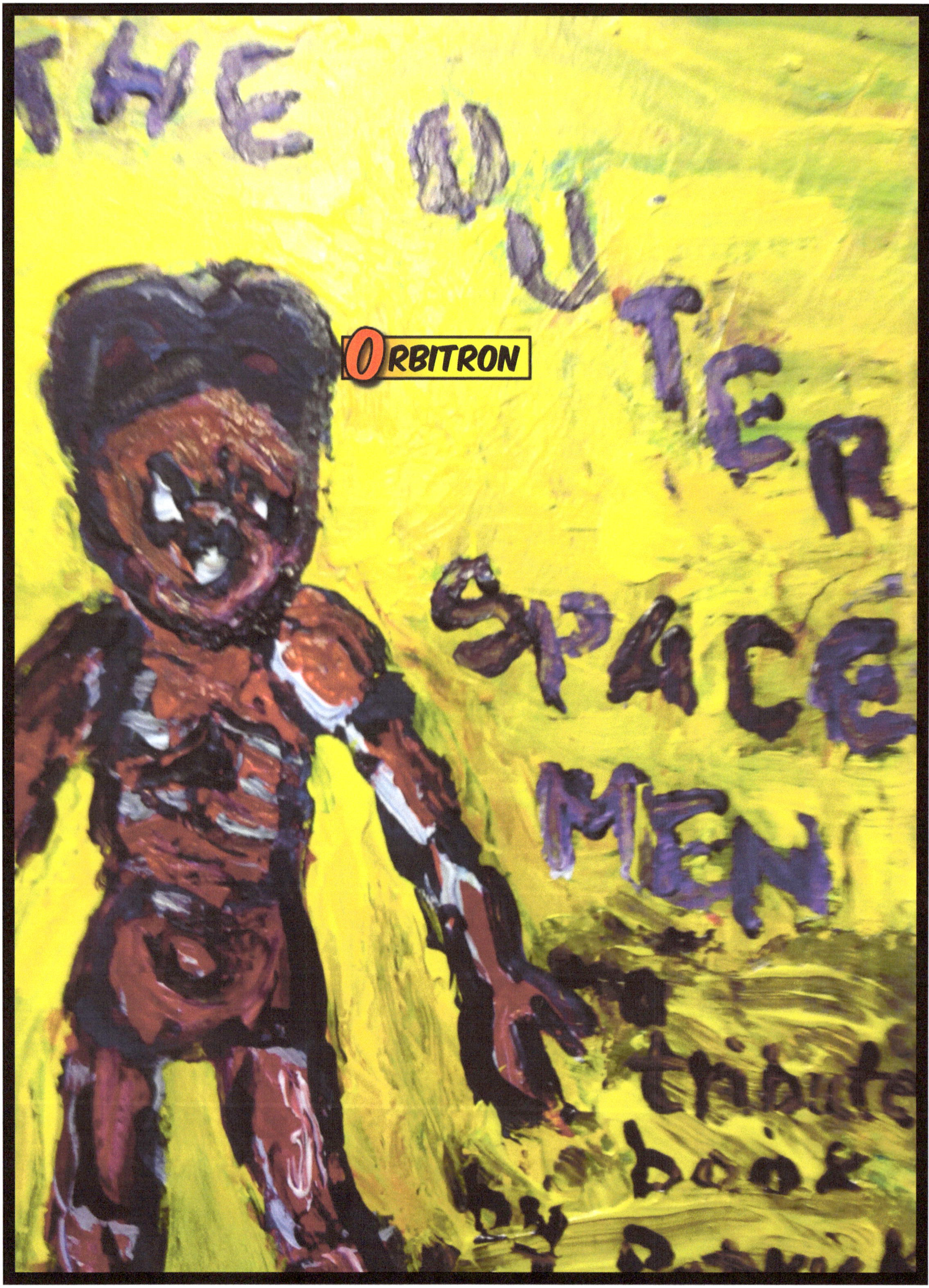
THE OUTER SPACE MEN
ORBITRON
a tribute book by

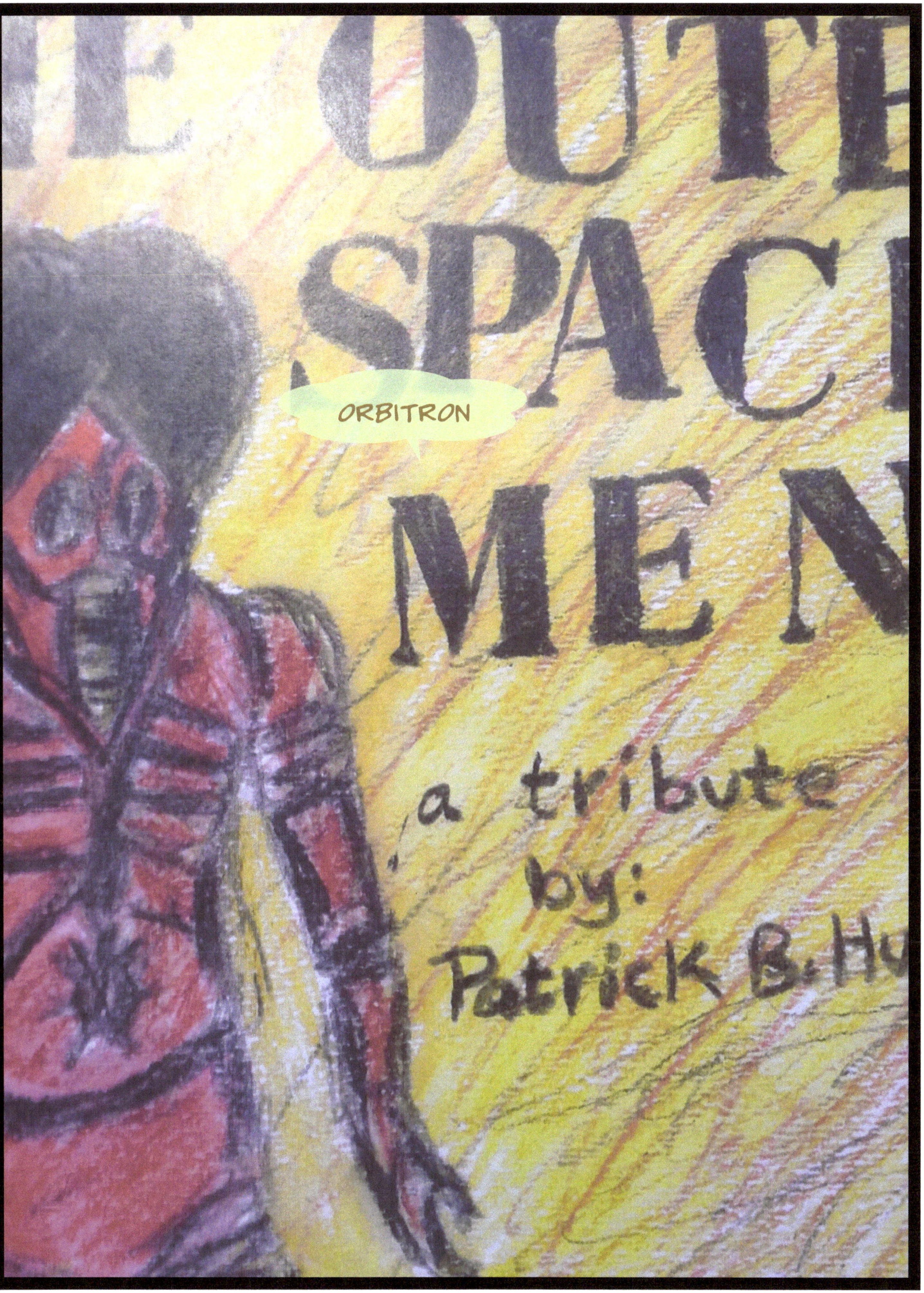
HE OUTE
SPAC
MEN
ORBITRON
a tribute
by:
Patrick B. Hu

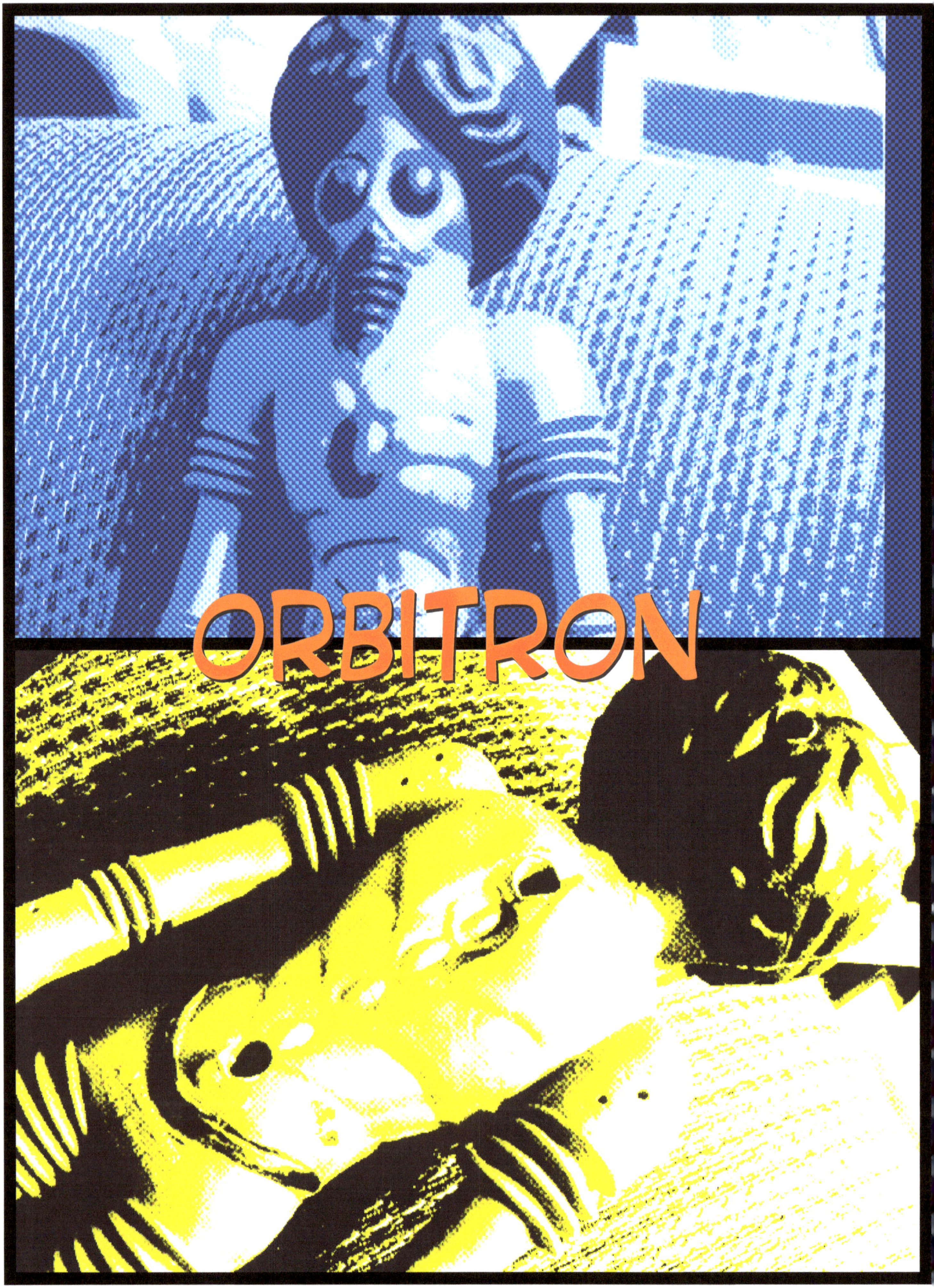
ORBITRON

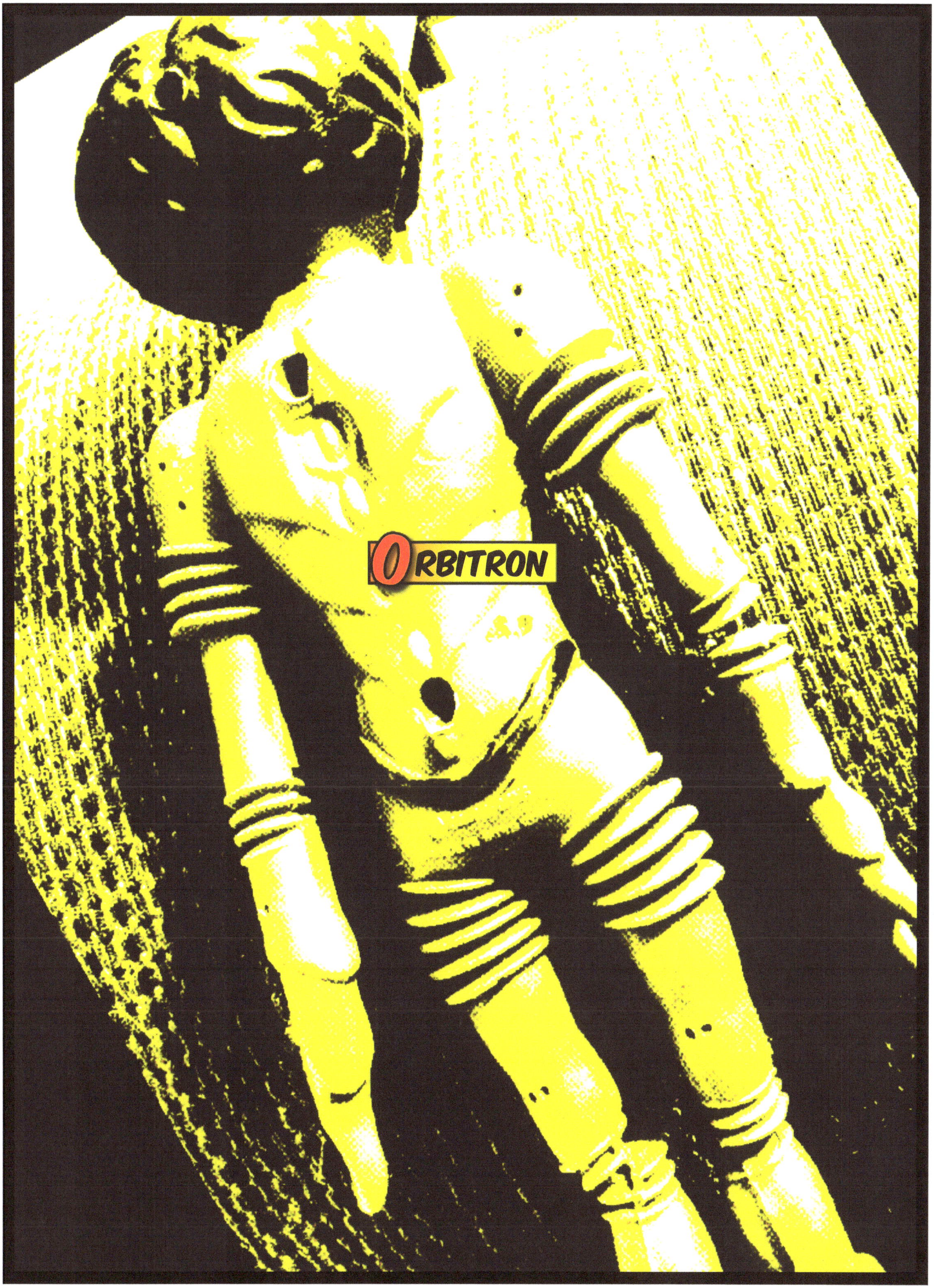
ORBITRON

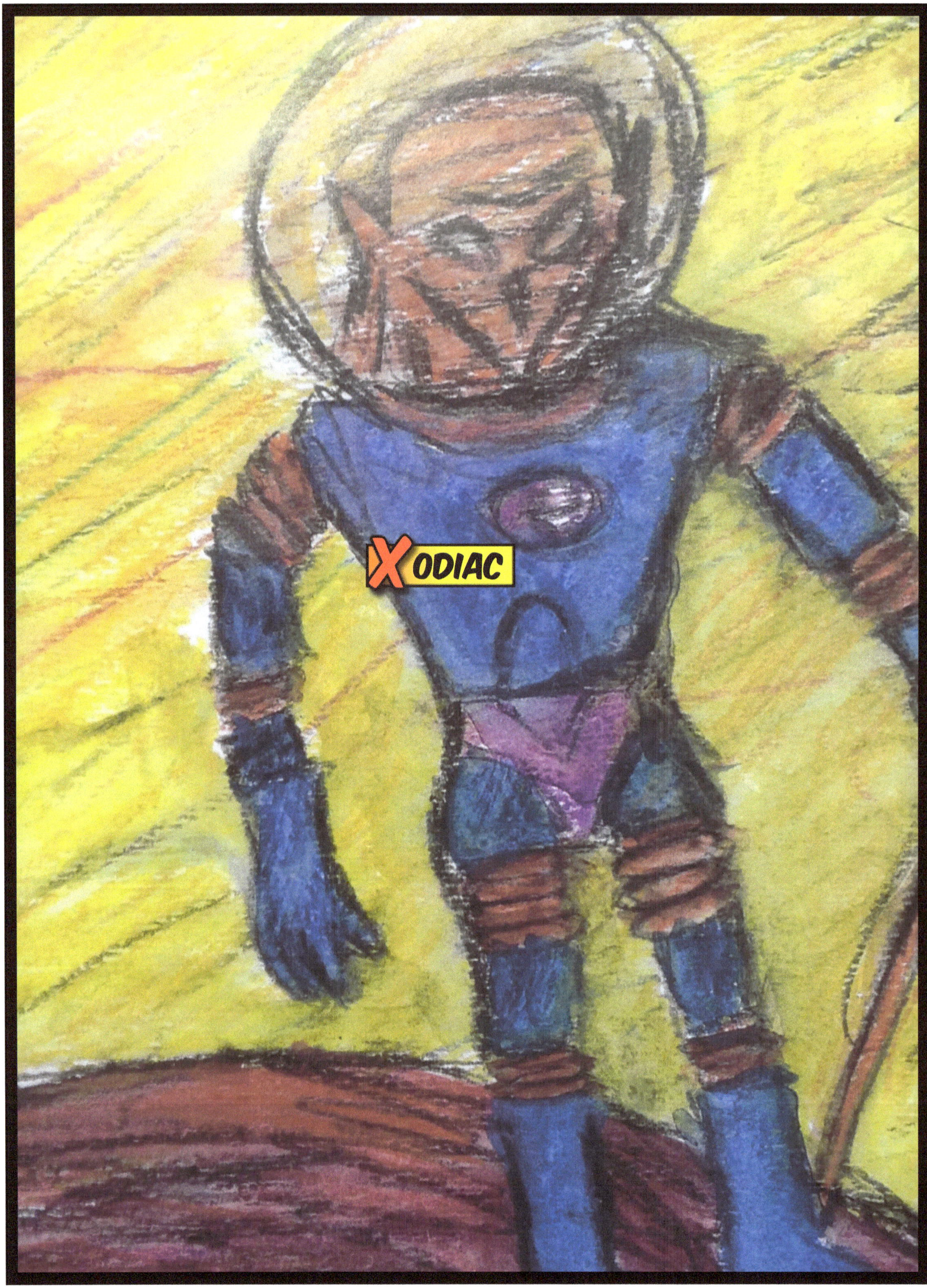
XODIAC

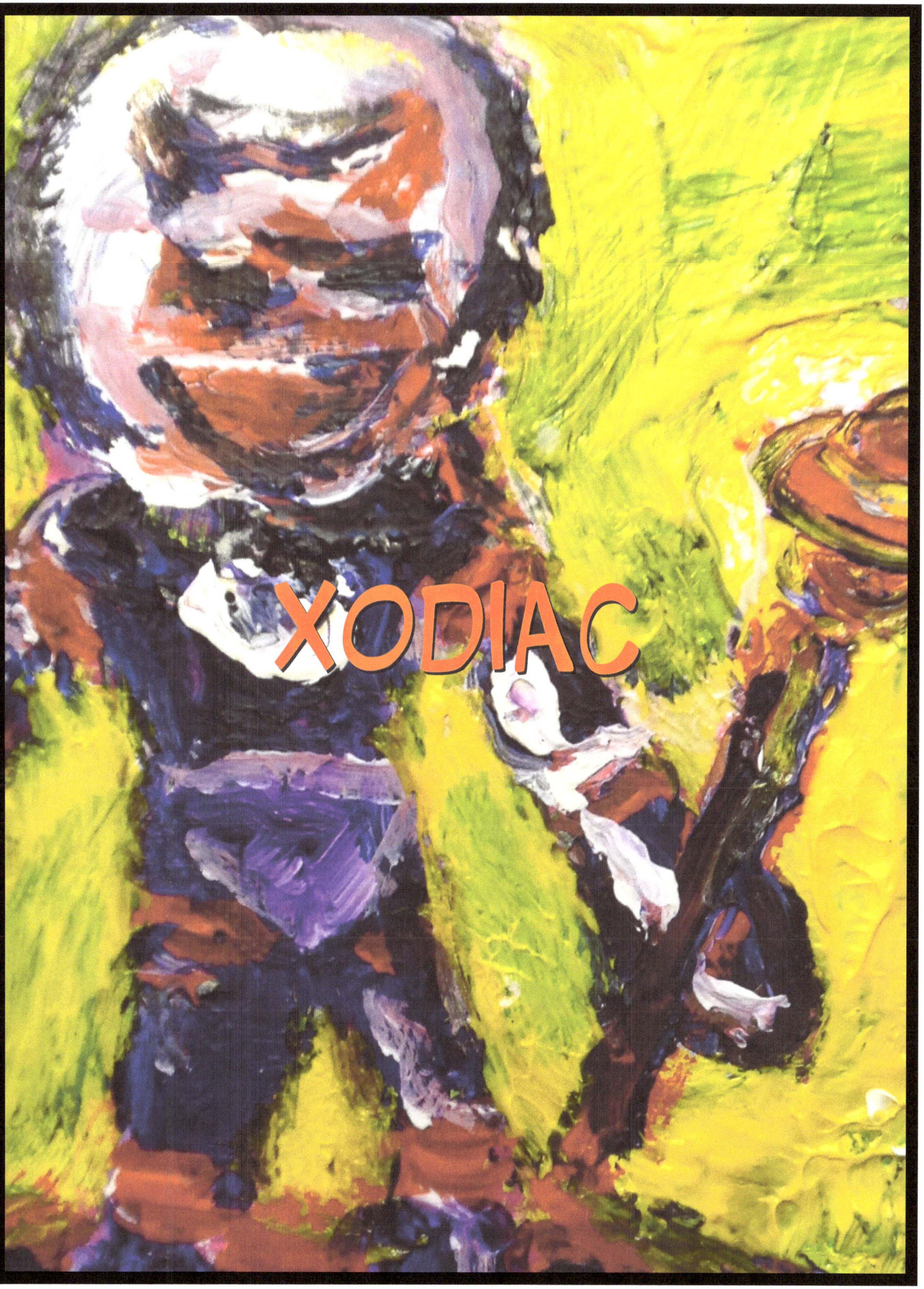
XODIAC

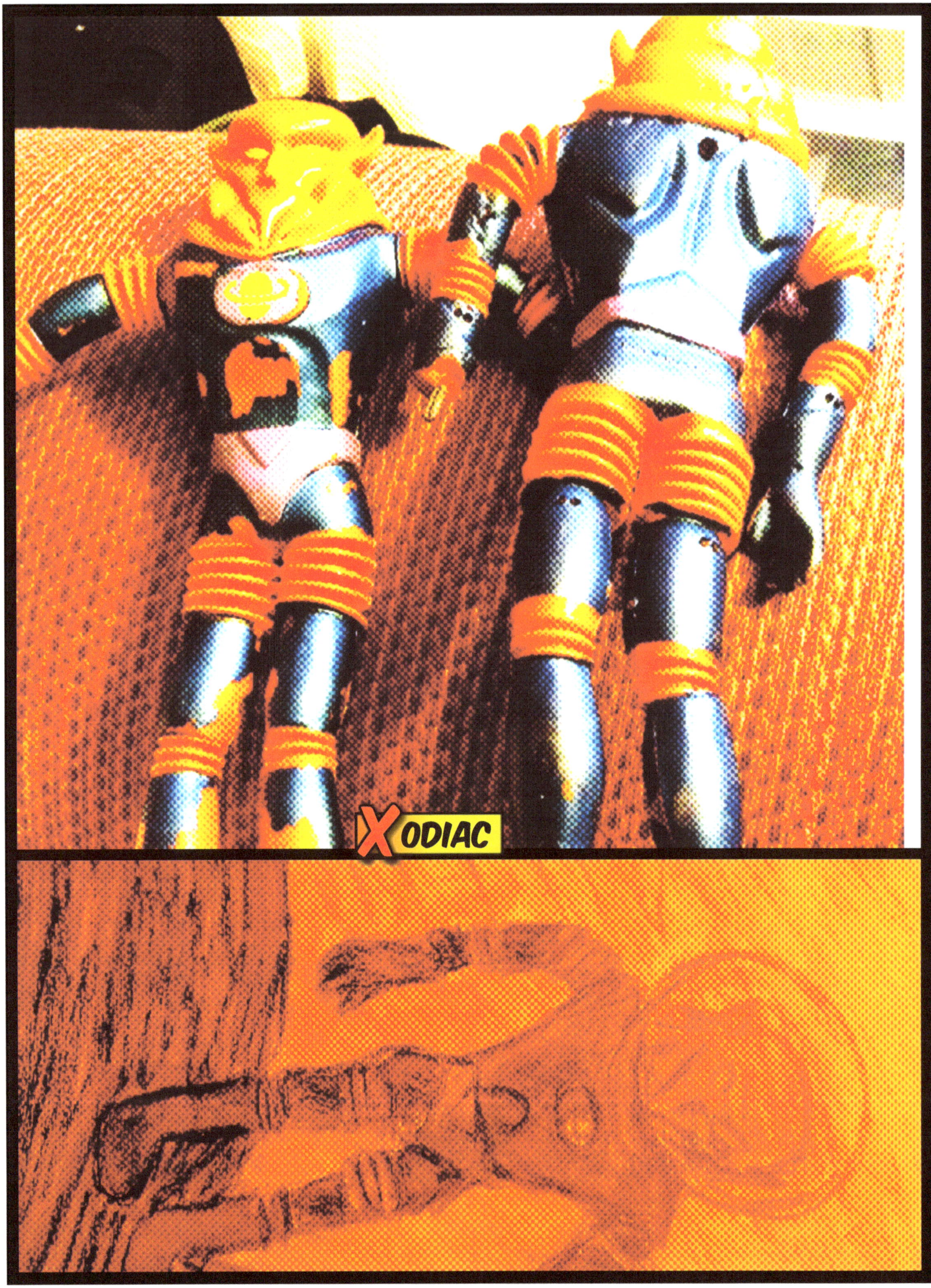
XODIAC

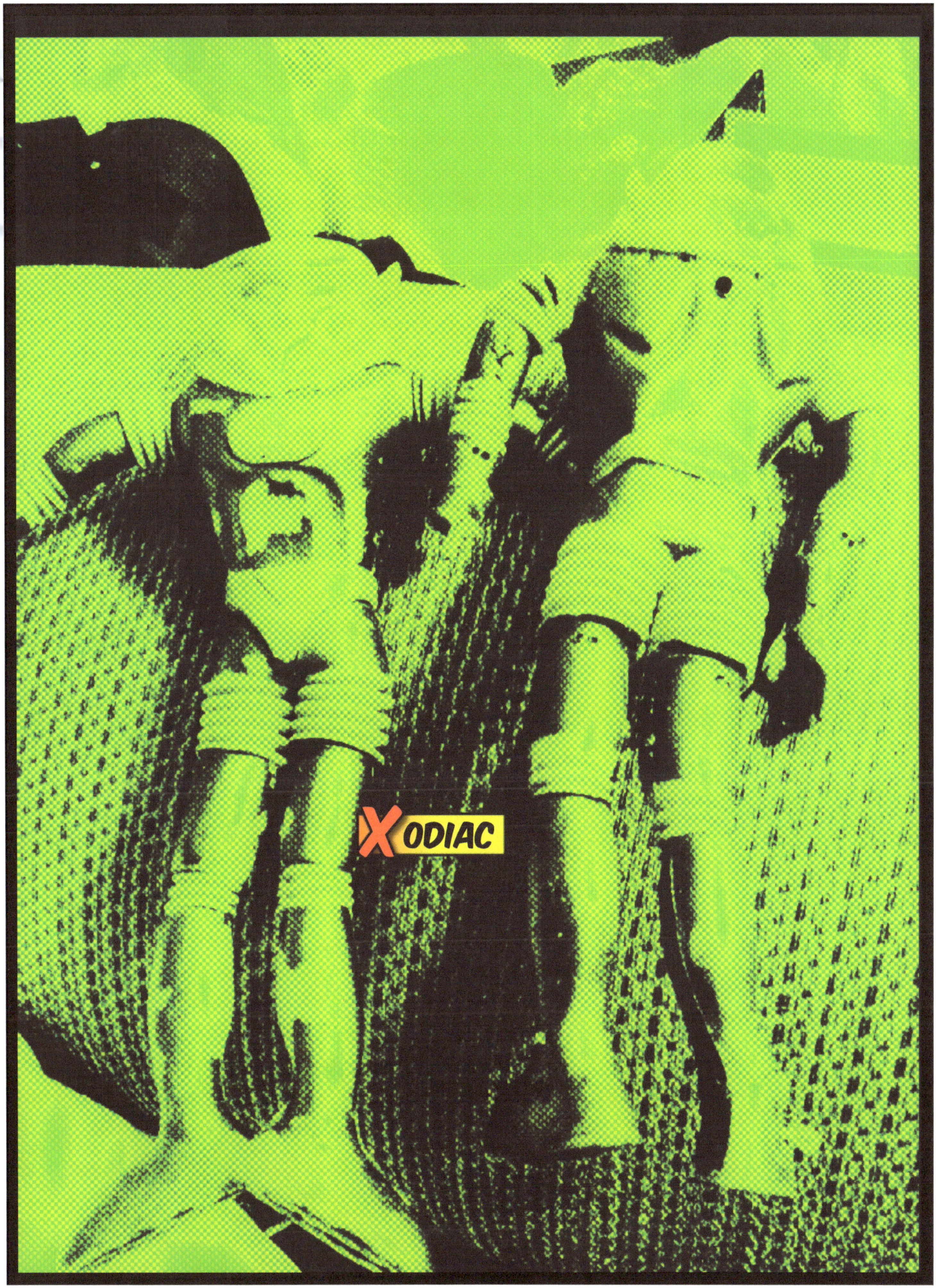
XODIAC

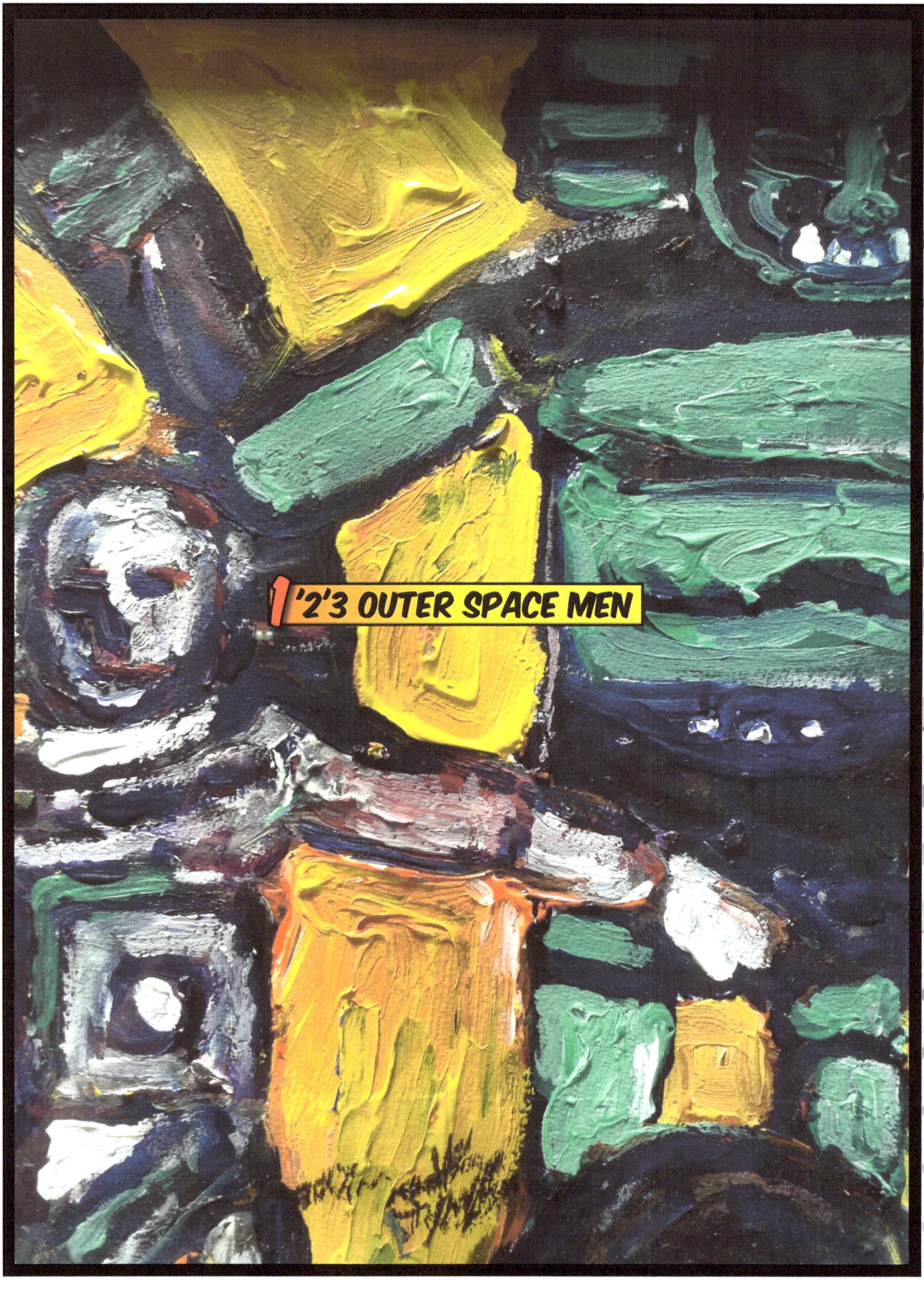
1'2'3 OUTER SPACE MEN

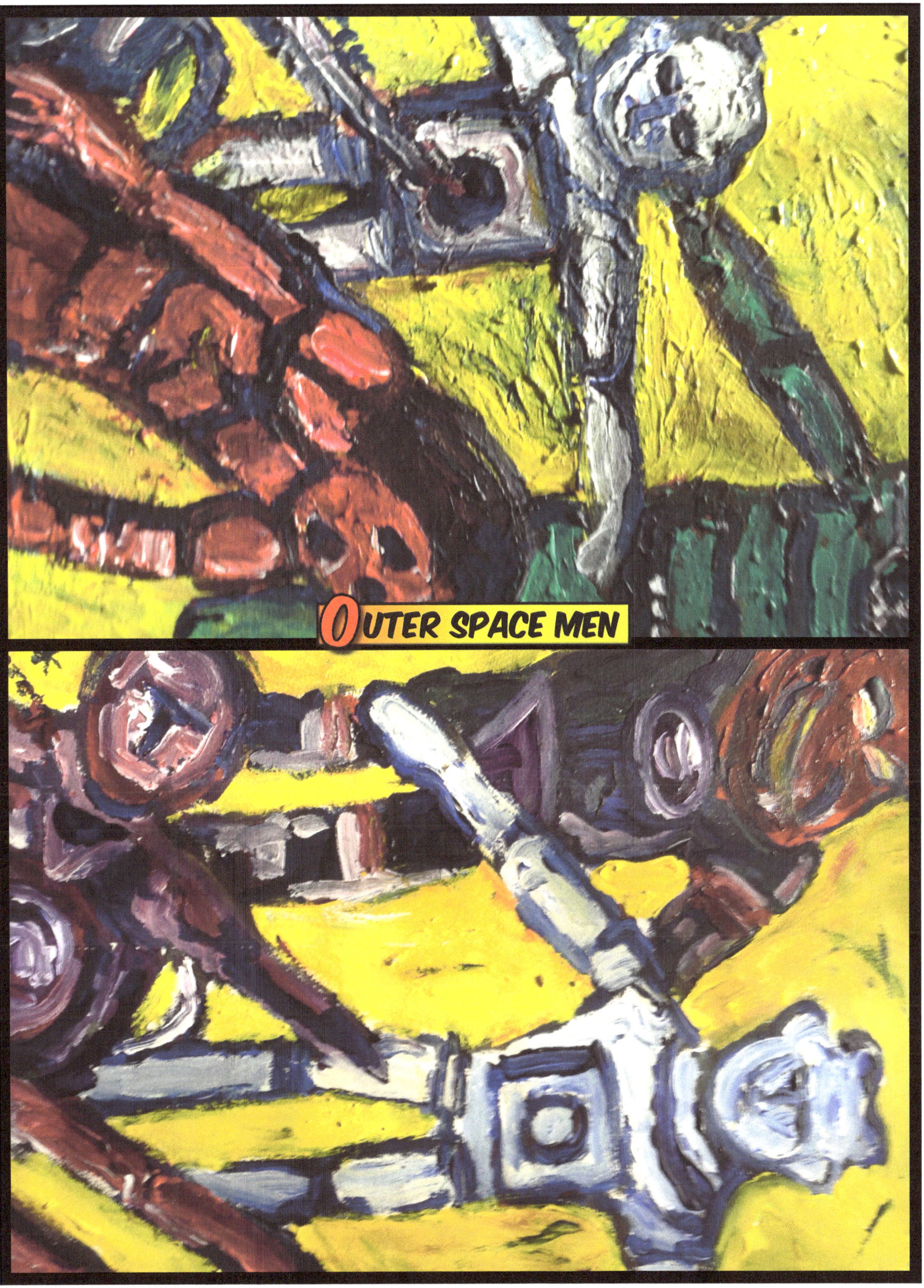
OUTER SPACE MEN

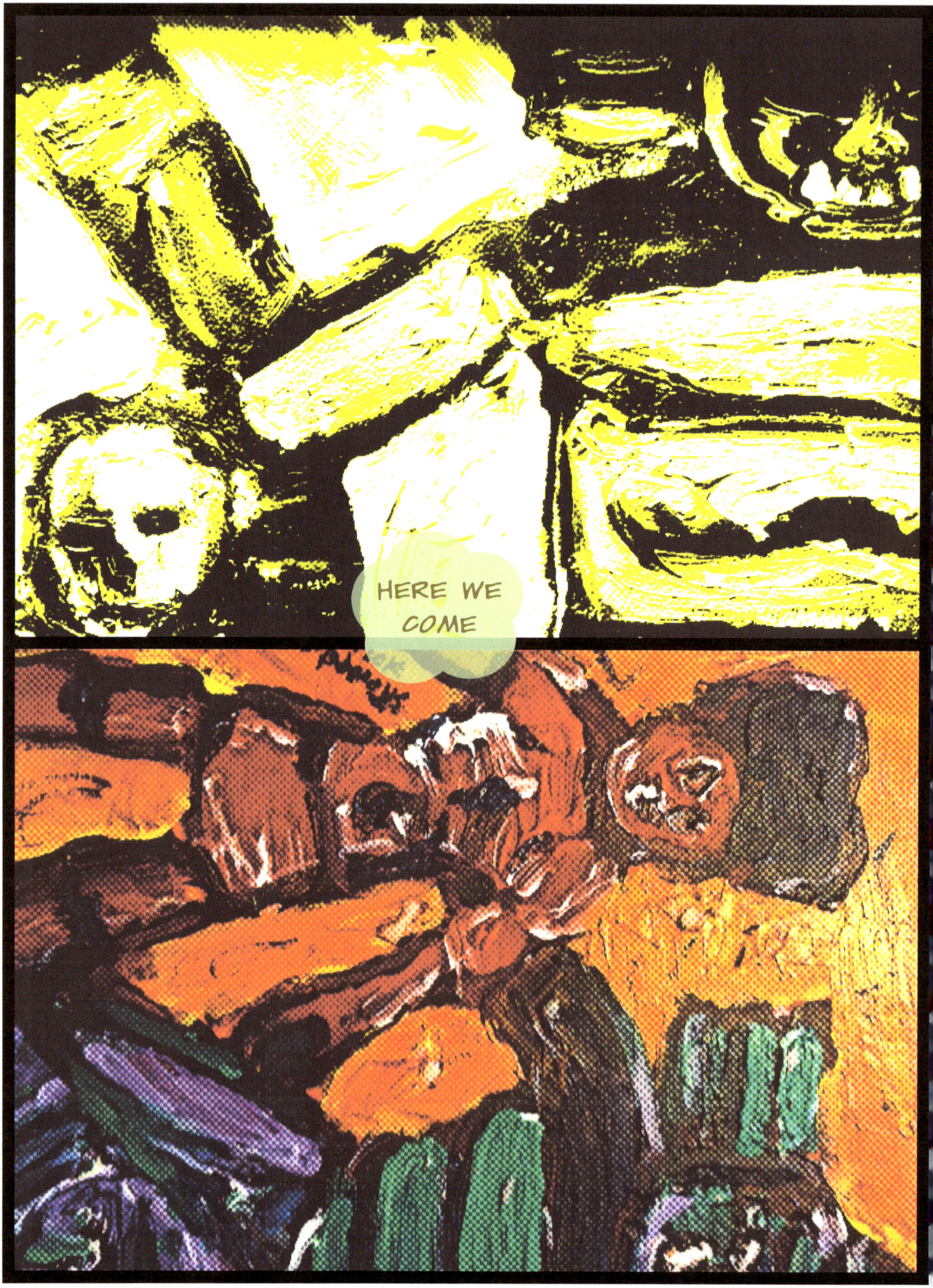
HERE WE COME

www.ingramcontent.com/pod-product-compliance
Lightning Source LLC
Chambersburg PA
CBHW050426180526
45159CB00005B/2433
9781484192870